A Collector's Guide

Teddy Bears

JUDITH MILLER

FIREFLY BOOKS

A FIREFLY BOOK

Published by Firefly Books Ltd. 2010

First printing

Publisher Cataloging-in-Publication Data (U.S.)
A CIP record of this book is available from Library of Congress

Library and Archives Canada Cataloguing in Publication
Miller, Judith, 1951-
            A collector's guide to teddy bears / Judith Miller.
Includes index.
ISBN-13: 978-1-55407-777-9
ISBN-10: 1-55407-777-X
            1. Teddy bears. 2. Teddy bears--History. I. Title.
NK8740.M45 2010   745.592'43   C2010-902186-X

Published in the United States by
Firefly Books (U.S.) Inc.
P.O. Box 1338, Ellicott Station
Buffalo, New York 14205

Published in Canada by
Firefly Books Ltd.
66 Leek Crescent
Richmond Hill, Ontario L4B 1H1

Printed in China

Front cover: A Steiff bear, with early blank ear button, c1905.

Set in Myriad Pro

Colour reproduction by United Graphics, Singapore
Printed and bound in China by Toppan

Consultants: Leanda Harwood, Peter Woodcock and Mark Hill

Publishing Manager: Julie Brooke
Editor: Davida Saunders
Editorial Assistant: Katy Armstrong

Design: Jeremy Tilston

Indexer: Diane Lecore

Production: Peter Hunt, Lucy Carter & Susan Meldrum

A Collector's Guide to

Teddy Bears

Contents

Introduction

W|e all love teddy bears. Considering the number of well-loved friends I see on the Antiques Roadshow, teddies are still treasured by collectors of all ages. My own Merrythought bear is still with me, in pride of place in the bedroom, although rather play-worn befitting his much-loved status. In fact I feel rather sad when shown an old teddy in pristine condition as it has obviously not had enough fun.

'Alfonzo', a rare early Steiff coloured teddy bear.

Teddy bears evoke the nostalgia of childhood more than any other toy. But there's more to it than that. There is that precious moment when you buy a second bear to keep your own bear company… and then a third. At that point you have become a collector. We collectors are obsessive and learning to distinguish the different makers and dates can lead to exciting finds in brocantes in Brittany and car boot sales in Cardiff!

A Farnell bear, c1925.

A 1920s/30s Schuco bear miniature manicure set.

With the publicity surrounding world record prices for old bears, fakes have appeared on the market. One of the best ways to identify a genuine old bear is to sniff it… it is impossible to fake that much-loved smell.

Although, of course, collectors are always on the look-out for that early Steiff in a rare colour, a bear with an appealing expression or a quizzical air will always find a good home. The 'but I couldn't resist him' is particularly relevant when it comes to bears – as is evidenced in the pages of this book.

A Merrythought 'Punkinhead' bear, c1951.

Judith Miller.

PRICE CODES

The price codes featured in this book are based on the prices realized at auction or asked by vintage bear dealers. They should be used as a guide only.

☆☆☆☆☆☆	£5,000/$7,500+
☆☆☆☆☆	£2,000–5,000/$3,000–7,500
☆☆☆☆	£1,000–2,000/$1,500–3,000
☆☆☆	£500–1,000/$750–1,500
☆☆	£100–500/$150–750
☆	<£100/$150

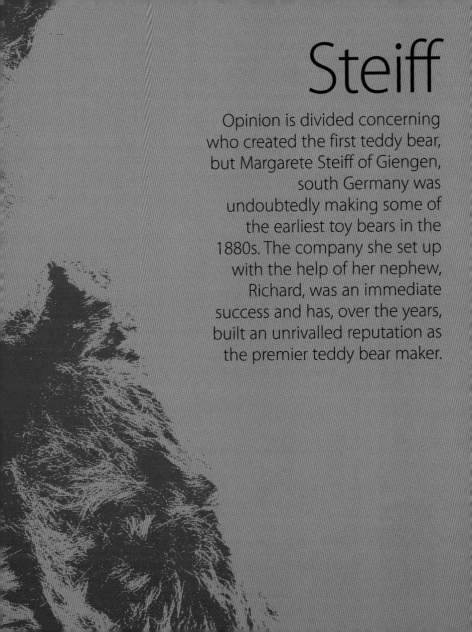

Steiff

Opinion is divided concerning who created the first teddy bear, but Margarete Steiff of Giengen, south Germany was undoubtedly making some of the earliest toy bears in the 1880s. The company she set up with the help of her nephew, Richard, was an immediate success and has, over the years, built an unrivalled reputation as the premier teddy bear maker.

◀ *An early Steiff plush teddy bear with metal rod joints, and a sealing-wax nose, with the elephant-shaped button in ear. 1904 18in (45.5cm) high* ☆☆☆☆☆

▲ *A Steiff cinnamon mohair teddy bear, with blank metal button in ear. c1906 16in (40.5cm) high* ☆☆☆☆☆

▲ *A Steiff bear-on-wheels, with original collar and bell, worn fur, non-working squeaker, and blank button. 1905–06 16in (40.5cm) high* ☆☆☆☆

"Teddy bears go everywhere and do everything."

MARGARET HUTCHINGS

▲ *A Steiff bear-on-wheels, with jointed head, ear button, burlap fur. 1900–10 16in (40.5cm) high ☆☆☆☆*

Margarete Steiff

The Steiff motto is 'only the best is good enough for our children'. Famous for their innovative designs, appealing shapes, attention to detail, and superb quality, Steiff are, arguably, the top manufacturers of teddy bears, the Rolls Royce of the trade. Like that famous car, Steiff teddy bears are not cheap. *All* of the world's most valuable bears have been Steiff bears, including 'Teddy Girl', a 1904 cinnamon mohair bear who sold for £110,000 in 1905 (see pages 68–9), and the 'Louis Vuitton' bear, made and sold in 2000, for £130,000.

Steiff was founded in 1877 by a remarkable woman, Margarete Steiff (1847–1909). Crippled with polio during childhood and confined to a wheelchair, she studied needlework and opened a clothing shop. She also began making stuffed toys using left-over felt from her uncle's fabric factory, which her brother sold. As her soft toy business grew in popularity many of her family joined her, including her nephew, Richard. It was Richard who introduced jointed bears, based on sketches he had drawn during his visits to Stuttgart Zoo.

The first jointed bear, the 55PB, was exhibited in 1903 at the Spring Fair in Leipzig and met with minimal success. Richard continued to work on design, producing a smaller, less plump bear, with improved joints and light mohair plush. Registered in 1904 as the Bär (bear) 35 PB, the new bear met with great acclaim and instant popularity. By the end of the year, 12,000 had been sold. In 1907, later called the year of the bear, Steiff sold nearly a million bears.

Margarete Steiff died in 1909, having seen her business become an astonishing success, leaving her uncles and nephews to continue to build the company.

◀ *A rare Steiff white mohair teddy bear, with original felt pads, boot button eyes and light brown, stitched nose, blank metal button in ear, in excellent condition. c1906 12.5in (32cm) high* ☆☆☆☆☆

▶ *A white Steiff bear, with button, and original light-coloured nose stitching.*
c1906–07
9in (25cm) high
☆☆☆

"Once a bear has been loved by a human being, its expression is forever marked."

JAMA KIM RATTIGAN

▲ *A Steiff small brown mohair bear, missing button in ear. c1907*
10in (25.5cm) high ☆☆☆

◄ *A Steiff blonde mohair bear, missing button-in-ear. c1907–10*
9.75in (25cm) high
☆☆☆☆

▲ *A Steiff teddy bear, with pad feet, some exposed straw, stitched woollen nose and claws, boot button eyes. c1907 13in (33cm) high* ☆☆☆☆

▲ 'Chester', a Steiff teddy bear, dressed in a sailor suit, with miniature bear in pocket, both with later trademark button-in-ear. This bear is especially valuable because of its rare period accessories and mint condition. 1907 10in (25.5cm) high ☆☆☆☆☆☆

► An early Steiff cinnamon plush bear, with button-in-ear, with boot button eyes and stitched snout, growler not working, paw pads replaced, repairs to foot pads. c1908 13in (33cm) high ☆☆☆☆

Alfonzo

In 1908 Grand Duke George Michailovitch (1863–1919) gave his daughter, Princess Xenia (1903–1965) a small, red Steiff bear, with solid black boot button eyes, a black stitched nose and cream pads. Soon afterwards the princess's nanny, Miss Bourne, known in the family as 'Nanabell', made the bear a Cossack outfit, which he still wears today.

Xenia named the bear 'Alfonzo', meaning noble, prompt, and ready for struggle. Unfortunately, Alfonzo and Xenia would soon have many struggles to face.

In 1914 Xenia and Alfonzo went to Buckingham Palace to stay with her mother's cousin George V and Queen Mary. The outbreak of the First World War prevented their return to Russia. When the Russian Revolution began in 1917 it became evident they would need to remain in London for even longer, so Xenia, her mother and her bear moved to their own house in Chester Square in Belgravia. In 1918 Tsar Nicholas II and his family were shot dead. Xenia's father escaped, but was assassinated the following year in St Petersburg. Alfonzo, Xenia's last memento of her father, became dearer to her than ever and remained a treasured possession for the rest of her life.

Alfonzo remained in the family until Xenia's daughter, Nancy (1926-2006), took him to Christie's in New York in 1988. He came up for sale at Christie's South Kensington, London, saleroom in 1989, with an estimate of £6,000, but fetched twice as much, selling for £12,100 – then the highest price ever paid for a teddy bear – to Ian Pout of Teddy Bears of Witney, where he can be seen today.

◀ *'Alfonzo', a rare early Steiff coloured teddy bear, with period clothes. 1908*
13in (33cm) high ☆☆☆☆☆

"In our childhood, teddy bears are warm companions – good listeners, never critical, always reassuring."

PEGGY AND ALAN BIALOSKY

▲ *A Steiff blonde mohair bear, with original pads, black boot button eyes, and woven nose, in extremely clean condition. c1908 13in (33cm) high* ☆☆☆☆

▶ *A Steiff bear, with button-in-ear and original black glass eyes. c1908 9.5in (24cm) high* ☆☆☆

◀ *A white Steiff bear, with typical hump back and long limbs, felt pads, boot button eyes, no ear button, in well-loved condition. 1908 12in (30.5cm) high* ☆☆☆

▶ *A Steiff gold mohair bear, in good condition,
no button, felt paws. c1909 13in (33cm) high* ☆☆☆

▲ A Steiff somersaulting bear. The arms are wound forward, as if winding a clockwork toy, to provide the momentum for a somersault. c1909 12in (30.5cm) high ☆☆☆☆

◀ *A Steiff blonde mohair teddy bear, of typical early form, with felt pads, woven nose and black boot button eyes. c1910 17in (43cm) high* ☆☆☆☆☆

▲ *A Steiff Rattle Bear, with white mohair and black glass eyes, body stuffed with wood shavings and a metal rattle. 1912 3in (7.5cm) high* ☆☆☆

"Teddy bears like to go on morning picnics, so they can enjoy the sunshine before it is too hot for their furry selves."

ABIGAIL DARLING

▲ *A brown Steiff bear, with green ribbon and button-in-ear, in fine condition. This model is unusual in this colour. c1920 18in (46cm) high* ☆☆☆☆☆

◀ *An early-mid 1920s Steiff bear, the pads worn, with working growler. 16.5in (42cm) high* ☆☆☆☆

◀ *A Steiff blonde bear, with button-in-ear and remnant of a tag, in good condition. 1927–34 11.75in (30cm) high* ☆☆☆☆

◀ *A rare, large Steiff 'Teddy Clown' bear, with large glass eyes set close together, body filled with kapok stuffing, and still complete with label. This bear was made in pink, gold or brown-tipped mohair plush and sold in 11 different sizes, from 9in (23cm) to 45in (114cm) tall. Only 30,000 were made by Steiff between 1926 and 1928.*
☆☆☆☆☆☆

35

▶ *A late 1920s Steiff bear with a strong provenance, with button-in-ear, wearing a pottery bead necklace from its original owner, the growler broken. This bear also has two dresses and a quilt from its original owner. 19in (48cm) high*
☆☆☆☆☆

▲ *A Steiff blonde mohair teddy bear, with early face, original pads, woven nose and black boot button eyes. 1920s 17in (43cm) high* ☆☆☆☆

▼ *A 1930s/40s small Steiff bear, with button-in-ear, in good condition. 5.25in (13.5cm) high* ☆☆

◀ *A 1950s Steiff Original Teddy, with button-in-ear but tag missing. The Original Teddy design was created in 1951. 13.5in (24.5cm) high*
☆☆

"Even though there is a rip in your teddy bear, his love will not fall out."

EVE FRANCES GIGLIOTTI

▲ *A Steiff bear, with button-in-ear, wearing a red ribbon. c1950s 3.25in (8.5cm) high* ☆☆

◄ *A chocolate brown Steiff 'Teddy Baby', with button-in-ear. c1950s 3.5in (9cm) high* ☆☆

▲ *A 1950s Steiff 'Zotty', bear, with characteristic peach-coloured bib, in excellent condition. 'Zotty' bears were introduced by Steiff in 1951 and are named after the German word for shaggy, 'zottig,' in reference to their long hair. The designs were widely copied by other makers. 12in (30.5cm) high* ☆

▶ *A 1950s rare white Steiff 'Zotty', with peach fur to bib. 12in (30.5cm) high* ☆☆

"My teddy was there when I had no friends to play with..."

ROBERT KUNCIOV

◀ *A Steiff 'Zooby Zoo' bear. 1954–60 10.5in (26.5cm) high ☆☆*

◀ *A 1950s Steiff blonde bear, missing button-in-ear. 20in (51cm) high ☆☆*

▲ *A 1950s white Steiff miniature bear. 3.5in (9cm) high* ☆

▲ *A Steiff 1950s miniature bear, from the 'Original Teddy' range, with bright golden mohair and original red ribbon, no button-in-ear. 5.25in (13.5cm) high* ☆

▶ *A 1950s Steiff white mohair miniature 'Teddy Baby', with velour face and feet.*
3.5in (9cm) high
☆☆

> *"Does Tussah Bear have a philosophy on life? I think so. It's something like, 'Love hard and only one person, and never leave them alone'."*
>
> JENNIFER PAULSON

▲ *A probably 1960s small Steiff teddy bear, with a replaced tag to the ear. 5.25in (13.5cm) high*☆☆

▶ *A 1960s/70s Steiff bear, with Steiff tag in ear. 7.5in (19cm) high* ☆

▶ *A 1970s Steiff 'Minky Zotty', with art-plush fur and growler. 10in (25.5cm) high* ☆

Ideal and early American bears

President 'Teddy' Roosevelt is credited as the inspiration behind the first bear, after he was reported to have refused to shoot a bear cub tied to a tree while out hunting in 1902. The Ideal Novelty and Toy Co. is believed to have produced the first American 'teddy' bears a year later in 1903, with other companies quick to take advantage of a new trend in the years following.

◀ *An early American bear, with 'sliced-in' ears and a humped back. Sliced-in ears are slotted in to the seams during making. 1905-06 18in (46cm) high* ☆☆

"Long before I grew up, my teddy bear taught me what love really meant – being there when you're needed."

JIM NELSON

▲ *A scarce and early gold mohair American teddy bear, with black boot button eyes, original felt pads, woven nose and claws. The triangular shape of this bear's head and snout suggest he may be by the American maker Ideal. c1905-1910 24.5in (62cm) high*
☆☆☆☆☆

▲ *An American bear-on-wheels, with fixed head position, retaining tail. American bears-on-wheels are unusual because they were less successful there than in Germany, where performing bears were an established tradition, so fewer were produced. 1900-10 16in (40.5cm) high* ☆☆

◀ *An unidentified American bear, with boot button eyes, black wool stitched nose and fabric pads. 1906-08 12.5in (32cm) high* ☆☆☆

▶ *An American*
Hecla bear. c1907
15in (38cm) high
☆ ☆ ☆ ☆

▶ *An American Hecla bear with glass eyes. c1907 12in (30.5cm) high*
☆☆☆☆

▲ An early American bear, with no markings or buttons. Many bears were made in the US in the early 20thC when they were new and fashionable, and they were often produced without labels, making them difficult to identify. Short feet or feet that come to a point are typical features of early American bears, as are rounder ears set low down on the head. c1908 10in (25.5cm) high ☆☆

"A bear teaches us that if the heart is true, it doesn't matter much if an ear drops off."

HELEN EXLEY

▲ *An early American bear, with pointy feet. c1908 11.5in (29cm) high* ☆☆

▲ *An American blonde mohair bear, with boot button eyes and stitched black wool nose and mouth. 1906-08 11.5in (29cm) high* ☆☆☆

◀ *An early American pale gold plush 'pinched ear' bear, with boot button eyes, paw pads re-covered in chamois. c1910 20in (51cm) high* ☆☆☆

Ideal

The Ideal Novelty and Toy Company was founded in 1903 by Morris Michtom and his wife Rose. The couple were allegedly responsible for creating the first teddy bear, based on the famous Clifford Berryman cartoon of President Roosevelt's encounter with a bear cub.

Early Ideal bears had wide triangular heads with large round ears, feet that taper to a point, short mohair and Excelsior stuffing, consisting of thinly shredded wood, also known as 'wood wool'. Several are similar in style to bears made by Steiff. Most early Ideal bears had black boot button eyes, but Ideal also produced some bears with painted white-rimmed boot button eyes. It was one of these 'googly-eyed' bears that was reputedly thrown from the back of a train by Teddy Roosevelt during his election campaign in 1904.

After the First World War, Ideal, like most other American manufacturers, switched to glass eyes. The body shape also changed, becoming rounded, with shorter limbs and small feet.

Morris Michtom died in 1938 and the company was taken over by his son, Benjamin, who introduced new designs and materials. The company became known as the Ideal Toy Company and began to mark its bears with a stitched label and paper tag in the shape of a circus wagon. During the 1950s, Ideal made a number of bears with realistic-looking, soft moulded-vinyl faces.

Ideal became a public company in 1968 and continued to make bears, character dolls and other animals until 1984.

◀ *An American Ideal blond mohair teddy bear, with original eyes, stitched nose and paw pads. This bear shows a number of features typical of Ideal's bears, including a triangular head, and ears widely spaced apart and set on the sides of the head. Arms set low on the body are another typical feature. c1910 13in (33cm) high ☆☆*

▲ *A 1920s American bear, with glass eyes and good quality mohair.*
16in (40.5cm) high ☆☆

"No one with one ounce of sensitivity could ever consign a bear to the dustbin."

JOHNNIE HAGUE

▲ *A 1920s American Ideal cinnamon mohair plush bear, with large flat feet, felt paw pads, triangular head, small amber-coloured glass eyes and a long snout. 15in (38cm) high* ☆☆☆

Colonel Bob Henderson

Teddy bear collector Colonel Bob Henderson was given his first bear – a Steiff cinnamon bear he named 'Teddy Girl' – when he was a baby in 1904. The bear accompanied him on active service and, after serving in World War II, Colonel Henderson dedicated his life to collecting bears. In 1962 he founded the Teddy Bear Club, and he later ran the UK branch of Good Bears of the World, a charity which sends teddy bears to children in need all over the world.

Good Bears of the World was founded in England in 1969 by the journalist James Theodore Ownby. It was based at his radio station in Honolulu, Hawaii, until 1991 when it moved to Toledo, Ohio. In 2009 it gave over 20,000 teddies to children in need around the world, including the victims of floods, tornadoes, hurricanes, and domestic violence. Bears were also given to many sick, injured and underprivileged children, as well as to lonely seniors.

'Teddy Girl' was sold at Christie's South Kensington, London, in December 1994 to Yoshihiro Sekiguchi, a businessman and founder of the Teddy Bear Museum in Izu, Japan. The cost? £110,000 – the highest price ever paid for a vintage bear.

◀ *A mid-20thC American teddy bear, named 'Boots' after his leather footwear. 'Boots' was given to Colonel Bob Henderson by an old lady with a note saying, 'Please look after my bear'. 16in (40.5cm) high* ☆☆☆☆☆

Farnell

It has been suggested that English company J.K. Farnell, established in 1840 as a firm making household goods, produced bears even before Steiff, but as few early Farnell bears have survived this has never been proved. Nevertheless, Farnell has been responsible for many wonderful English bears, including Christoper Robin's much-loved companion, Winnie-the-Pooh.

◀ A pre-World War I Farnell
bear. 14in (35.5cm) high
☆☆☆☆

▲ A Farnell 'mourning bear', these bears were made
to commemorate the sinking of the Titanic in 1912.
1912–14 14in (35.5cm) high ☆☆☆☆☆

▶ *The 'Hay' bear, probably by Farnell, dressed in the contemporary uniform of the Gordon Highlanders, in Hay tartan. This bear belonged to the son of Captain Hay, who fought in World War I. The uniform was made by the boy's nanny while his father was away fighting. 1915*
12in (30.5cm) high ☆☆☆☆☆

▶ *Three Farnell 'soldier bears'. These miniature bears by Farnell were often sold as gifts for sweethearts to take with them during World War I, their upturned faces allowing them to peek out of breast pockets. They were made in patriotic colours of red, white and blue, as well as the traditional gold colour. 1915 3.75in (9.5cm)* ☆☆ *each*

The Campbell Bears

These characterful little bears are part of a collection of 398 miniatures widely accepted to have been produced by Farnell. They belonged to twins David and Guy Campbell, born in 1910. The boys began collecting the bears one or two at a time, and used them to act out stories and adventures. When their grandmother discovered their passion, she also began buying bears by the dozen to add to the collection.

Once in the boys' hands the bears came alive, some even taking on names and personalities. These named bears were dressed in a 'uniform' of ribbons and sashes to identify them, and included 'Lord Wharton', the King of the Bears (opposite), named after an ancestor of the Campbell's.

◀ *A bear from the Campbell Collection, 'Lord Wharton', wearing a sash made from medal ribbon and a glass-topped hat pin 'sword' to indicate his position as King of the Bears.*
2.5in (6cm) high seated
☆☆☆☆☆

▶ *White and gold mohair bears from the Campbell Collection, dressed in strips of medal ribbon and felt.* ☆☆ *each*

▲ *A 1920s Farnell hand-puppet bear. 12in (30.5cm) high* ☆☆

▶ *A Farnell blonde mohair bear in mint condition, with glass eyes and webbed claws. c1918 16in (40.5cm) high* ☆☆☆☆

"A bedroom without a teddy is like a face without a smile."

GILL DAVIES

"Bears are just about the only toy that can lose just about everything and still maintain their dignity and worth."

SAMANTHA ARMSTRONG

◀ *A 1920s Farnell gold mohair bear, with webbed claws. 22in (56cm) high ☆☆☆☆*

▲ A Farnell white mohair bear, with ears set to the corners, a humped back, a rectangular vertically stitched nose, and webbed paw stitching. c1925 14in (35.5cm) high ☆☆☆☆

Farnell and Winnie-the-Pooh

J.K. Farnell was founded by John Kirby Farnell in 1840 in Notting Hill, London, and produced small household items, such as pin-cushions and tea cosies. The company began making soft toys at the end of the 19th century when Farnell's children, Agnes and Henry, took over the business.

In 1921, Agnes opened a second factory called The Alpha Works and in 1925 registered the Alpha trademark for all Farnell bears. One of the first bears made at the Alpha Works was bought in 1921 by English writer A.A. Milne for his son, Christopher Robin.

At first named simply 'Bear' or 'Teddy' (or 'Edward Bear' by adults), this bear soon acquired the name 'Winnie-the-Pooh' after Winnie, a North American bear which Christopher often saw at London Zoo, and 'Pooh', a swan they had met while on holiday. Now renamed, Winnie-the-Pooh began to appear in A.A. Milne's writing. Ernest Shepherd was commissioned to illustrate the stories, but though he based most of them on Christopher Robin's toys, Winnie-the-Pooh himself was primarily modelled on Shepherd's Steiff teddy.

Farnell continued to produce teddy bears until the 1960s, when Acton Toycraft took over the lease of Alpha Works and renamed it 'Twyford Works'.

◀ *A late 1920s Farnell bear, with short plush mohair and webbed claws, the growler broken. 25in (63.5cm) high* ☆☆☆☆

▶ *A 1920s white Farnell bear. 19in (48cm) high ☆☆☆☆*

"Here is Edward Bear, coming downstairs now, bump, bump, on the back of his head, behind Christopher Robin."

A.A. MILNE

◀ *A Farnell mohair 'Alpha' bear with original paw pads, black boot button eyes and stitched nose, slightly worn. c1930 9in (23cm) high* ☆☆

▲ *A 1920s blue Farnell bear. 9.25in (23.5cm) high* ☆☆☆☆

▲ *A small early 1930s Farnell 'Mascot Teddy', with card tag. 5in (12.5cm) high* ☆☆

▶ *A rare 1930s Farnell bear, made from alpaca, with minor restoration. Farnell used soft alpaca fur for its nursery range of bears for children up to around 5 years old. Alpaca fur often deteriorates over time but this bear is in excellent condition. 8in (20.5cm) high* ☆☆

"It is astonishing how many thoroughly mature, well-adjusted grown-ups harbour a teddy bear."

JOSEPH LEMPA

▲ *A 1940s Farnell bear, with orange mohair, in mint condition and unusually retaining the maker's label on the chest. 15in (38cm) high ☆☆*

Chiltern

Initially a doll maker, Chiltern's first bear, 'Master Teddy', was based on a character from the *Daily Mail's* 'Teddy Bear Tail League'. This characterful bear was the first of many innovative designs produced by Chiltern over the next 50 years, from the popular 'Hugmee' range to a range of bears in vibrant colours, to bears containing musical mechanisms including the famous 'Ting-a-ling'.

"The teddy bear, all things to all ages, all sizes for all preferences, symbol that all is right with the world if one only believes."

ANONYMOUS

▲ *A late 1930s Chiltern-type pale gold mohair plush bear, with glass eyes and worn Rexine paw pads. c1920 17in (43cm) high* ☆☆

◀ *A 1920s red teddy bear, possibly Chiltern. 27in (68cm) high*
☆☆☆☆☆

Chiltern

Chiltern Toys started life as a German toy export firm called Eisenmann & Co., founded by Josef and Gabriel Eisenmann in the late 19thC. In 1908 Josef opened the Chiltern Toy Works at Chesham, Buckinghamshire, with his son-in-law Leon Rees. The new company initially produced dolls, with the first bear made in 1915.

This bear, dubbed the 'Master Teddy' and made in five different sizes, was a comical-looking bear, with a large round head, small ears and big, glass 'googly' eyes. His nose had vertical stitching and his small, pink, felt tongue showed through his wide smile. Only the face, paws and feet of 'Master Teddy' were made from mohair, the rest of the body was made of cotton and dressed with a cotton jacket or shirt, and felt dungarees.

Leon Rees inherited the factory after Josef's death in 1919 and the following year began a partnership with Harry Stone, a former director of J.K. Farnell. Together they registered the name 'Chiltern Toys' in 1924. The firm's most famous range, the 'Hugmee' bear, was introduced the previous year.

During the 1930s there were innovations such as the 'Musical Bellows' bear, 'Silky Teddy' and the well-known 'Cubby' bear. During the war production was reduced, but in 1947 a new factory was opened in Pontypool, Wales, to cope with demand. More creations followed in the 1950s and 60s under chief designer Pamela Howells, such as the famous 'Teddy on a Bike' and the 'Ting-a-ling Bruin', which contained a mechanism that made a jingling sound.

In 1967, four years after the death of Leon Rees, Chiltern became a subsidiary of Chad Valley, and, for a short time, bears bore a 'Chad Valley Chiltern' label.

◀ *A Chiltern 'Master Teddy', wearing original clothes, with the early googly eyes. 1915 14in (35.5cm) high* ☆☆☆☆☆

▶ *A rare powder blue Chiltern bear. c1930 14.5in (37cm) high* ☆☆

◀ *A small Chiltern 'Ting-a-ling' teddy, with a bell in his tummy, velveteen pads, and a mark to the right foot where a label was once stitched on. c1940 12in (30.5cm) high ☆☆*

"A teddy bear will always care.
When all else fails hug your teddy."

ANONYMOUS

▲ A Chiltern 'Ting-a-ling' bear, with Rexine
foot pads, very worn with broken mechanism.
c1940 16in (40.5cm) high ☆

▶ *A 1930s/40s Chiltern bear. 20in (50.5cm) high* ☆☆

◀ *A 1930s Chiltern gold plush bear, with large glass eyes and velveteen paw pads. 25in (63.5cm) high*
☆☆☆

◀ *A gold mohair Chiltern bear. c1940s 12in (30.5cm) high* ✩✩

▲ *A Chiltern velvet mohair teddy bear, dressed as a Home Guard Sergeant, with a label on the foot that reads 'Chiltern Hygienic Toys made in England'. Few bears were produced during World War II, as teddy bear factories were expected to contribute to the war effort by producing necessities such as helmet linings. This bear was one of the few teddies produced at Chiltern during this time. c1940 12in (30.5cm) high* ☆☆

◀ *A Chiltern 'Hugmee' teddy bear, with original foot pads, woven nose, glass eyes and original tag. 1930s/40s 13in (33cm) high*☆☆

Hugmee

Launched in 1923, the 'Hugmee' is Chiltern's most famous range of teddy bears, named after the labels worn by early bears: 'Hug Me and I'll Growl'. So many variations of the Hugmee bear were produced between the 1920s and the 1960s (when the Hugmee was finally retired) that it is possible to build an interesting collection from these alone.

Most were made from golden mohair, but Hugmees were also produced in a range of pastel colours, including blue, pink, white and green and blonde. The early Hugmees typically had long, often shaved, muzzles, large thighs, long arms, a large tummy, bodies stuffed with kapok, heads stuffed with wood wool, and velvet or cotton paws and pads. The noses of early bears from the 1920s and 1930s have characteristic upward stitches at either side.

During and after World War II, materials became difficult to obtain so Chiltern changed the design of the Hugmee to use less fabric. Bears had shorter arms and legs and flatter faces. The nose stitching became shield-shaped without the long end stitches. The feet pads were made of Rexine, an imitation leather, which was often used on British bears of this period.

In the late 1950s and early 1960s, Hugmees were given plastic noses, reputedly taken from toy dogs that were being made in the factory at the same time. This nose was a success, especially as it conformed to the new safety regulations, and can be found on many of the later bears produced towards the final Chiltern years.

◀ *A Chiltern 'Hugmee' pale gold mohair plush bear, with velvet paw pads, amber and black glass eyes. 1950s 15in (38cm) high* ☆☆

▲ *A 1940s Chiltern gold mohair bear, with tag and in mint condition. Without the tag and in poorer condition this bear would be worth much less. 20in (50.5cm) high* ☆☆☆

▲ *A late 1940s-early 1950s Chiltern musical bear in excellent condition, with velveteen pads. Chiltern musical bears are less common. 16in (40.5cm) high* ☆☆

"At sales every other toy looks simply worn, dilapidated, grubby. A bear looks lost and abandoned and desperately in need of a loving home."

HELEN THOMPSON

▶ *A 1950s Chiltern 'Ting-a-ling Bruin' bear, with golden mohair and Rexine pads. The Ting-a-ling Bruin bear was introduced by Chiltern in the 1950s, and contained a mechanism that produced a musical tinkling sound when shaken. 12in (30.5cm) high ☆☆*

◀ *A late 1940s-early 1950s Chiltern 'Hugmee' bear, of a rare size, with card-lined feet and velveteen pads. 8in (20cm) high ☆☆*

▶ A Chiltern 'Hugmee' bear, dressed in a silk polka dot clown outfit of the same period, with label to right foot. This bear is one of the smaller sizes of the popular Hugmee range. c1950 10in (25.5cm) high ☆☆

▲ *A Chiltern musical 'Hugmee' bear with tag. Without the tag this bear would be worth much less. c1950s 16in (40.5cm) high* ☆☆☆

▲ *A 1950s Chiltern bear, with moulded plastic nose, and 'Chiltern Hygienic Toys' label in side seam, in good condition. It is unusual to find Chiltern Bears which retain their label. 10in (25.5cm) high* ☆☆

Q: "What should you call a bald teddy?"
A: "Fred bear."

ANONYMOUS

▲ *A Chiltern teddy bear, with glass eyes, plastic nose, jointed limbs and velveteen pads. Chiltern introduced plastic noses in the 1960s. 24in (61cm) high* ☆☆

▶ *A late 1960s Chad Valley Chiltern bear with tag. After Chiltern became a subsidiary of Chad Valley in 1967, bears were produced for a time with a label bearing the names of both companies. 11in (28cm) high* ☆☆

REAL
MOHAIR
LUXURY SOFT TOY
Chad Valley
Chiltern
MADE IN ENGLAND

Chad Valley

A printing business may seem an unlikely start for a toy maker, but Chad Valley began life as a stationers founded in 1820. The first bears were produced almost 100 years later in 1915, after success printing board games had led to the company's expansion into the toy market. In 1938 the company gained a Royal Warrant of Appointment as Toymakers to Her Majesty the Queen, and production flourished after the interruption of the Second World War.

"The world of
the teddy bear
is an innocent
one, a world
that gives delight
and hurts not."

GILES BRANDRETH

▲ A Chad Valley bear with early 'British Toys'
celluloid button to chest, and cork filled limbs.
1918 8in (20.5cm) high ☆☆

▶ *A Chad Valley bear, in excellent condition. c1919 10in (25.5cm) high* ☆☆

▲ A Chad Valley gold mohair plush teddy bear, with amber and black glass eyes, with metal identity button, wearing child's dress. 1930 26in (66cm) high ☆☆☆

▶ A 1930s Chad Valley 'Magna' bear, with label to right foot pad. The Magna series of bears was brought into production by Chad Valley around 1930. Magna bears have distinctive horizontal nose stitching. 20in (51cm) high ☆☆

◀ *A 1930s Chad Valley polar bear, with white mohair and down-turned paws, with Chad Valley label on left foot pad. 24in (61cm) high* ☆☆☆

▶ *A 1930s Chad Valley bear, with label on right foot pad. 23in (58.5cm) high* ☆☆☆

"How many
children have
carried a lifelong
resentment of
parents for
surreptitiously
removing their
teddy bears?"

JOHN ZIFF

Chad Valley

In the late 19th century Johnson Bros Ltd, a printing firm established in 1820, began producing games under the trademark Chad Valley, after the Chad stream that ran past their factory in Harborne, near Birmingham. Following the ban on German imports to Britain during World War I that affected established German bear makers such as Steiff and Bing, they produced their first jointed teddy in 1915. After patenting a stuffing machine they expanded their range to include a large variety of soft toys and bears, and moved to larger works in Shropshire in 1920, forming the Chad Valley Co. Ltd.

In 1938 the company was granted the Royal Warrant of Appointment as Toymakers. From then on, all their bears bore a label, typically on the foot, reading: 'Toymakers to Her Majesty the Queen'. When Queen Elizabeth II was crowned in 1953, the word 'Queen' was changed to 'Queen Mother'.

Chad Valley were among the first companies to use coloured mohair fabrics, and their first 'novel bear' was Rainbow Tubby Bear (1926) who wore a collar and a clown's hat. Chad Valley later made bears after famous characters, including Disney animals, Winnie-the-Pooh, Sooty and Toffee bear whose adventures featured in the BBC radio programme 'Listen With Mother'.

Production flourished, and Chad Valley took over other toy companies: Isaacs & Co in 1923, Peacock & Co. in 1931 and Chiltern Toys in 1967. The amalgamation with Chiltern created the largest soft-toy manufacturer in Great Britain, but the recession of the 1970s led to the shutting down of six of Chad Valley's seven factories, before Chad Valley was itself taken over by Palitoy in 1978.

◀ *A 1930s Chad Valley bear, with button and replaced pads. 15.5in (39.5cm) high* ☆☆

▲ *A 1930s English bear, probably Chad Valley, the mohair fur in very good condition. 20in (51cm) high* ☆☆

◀ *A large 1950s Chad Valley pale gold mohair plush bear, with typical wide nose, soft stuffed in parts, with label to left foot. 21in (53.5cm) high* ✩✩

▲ A 1930s Chad Valley white mohair plush bear, with Rexine paw pads, brown glass eyes, and remains of chest label. 17in (43cm) high ☆☆

▶ A late 1940s Chad Valley art silk musical bear, containing a Thorens musical mechanism. 14in (35.5cm) high ☆☆

On the tag:

CHAD VALLEY

hygienic

SOFT TOY

▲ *A large Chad Valley blonde mohair bear, with stitched nose, amber glass eyes, swivel-jointed body with Rexine pads and label on right foot. c1953 30in (76cm) high* ☆☆

▼ *A small Chad Valley teddy bear, with features characteristic of later Chad Valley bears, including the ears placed flat on the head, the bulbous nose stitched on vertically instead of horizontally, and longer and curved arms. c1950 12in (30.5cm) high* ☆☆

Sooty

Sooty is a silent but mischievous little bear, with a fondness for magic tricks, custard pie fights and squirting people (including Prince Philip) with his water pistol on British television. Joined by Sweep, a dog, and Soo, a panda, Sooty has delighted British children since 1948. It was then that comedian Harry Corbett first discovered the glove puppet for sale on Blackpool's North Pier for seven shillings and sixpence.

Corbett introduced the little bear into his amateur magic act, which included Sooty's favourite spell, 'Izzy Wizzy let's get busy!'. In 1952 the pair were spotted by a television producer and invited to appear on BBC North's 'Talent Night'. The puppet's nose and ears were hastily blackened with soot, so that he would show up better on black and white television, giving him his now famous name, Sooty.

The nation was captivated by Sooty and he received his own show in 1955, moving stations to ITV in 1964. Following Harry Corbett's retirement in 1976, Sooty was operated by his son Matthew and in 2000 Sooty passed to the young illusionist, Richard Cadell, who is still working with him today. Sooty's is now the longest-running children's programme in the UK and the bear has appeared on TV in Ireland, Australia, New Zealand and other countries.

Chad Valley were given the sole rights to manufacture Sooty in 1952 and they continued to produce him until 1980. No one knows where Harry Corbett's first Sooty is, but it is estimated that over a thousand puppets have been worn out in the shows since Sooty's debut.

◀ *A 1960s Chad Valley plush 'Sooty' teddy bear, wearing red dungarees. 10in (25.5cm) high* ☆

▶ A huge 1950s Chad Valley 'Bear Brand' shop-display bear. This bear was originally part of a display selling ladies' stockings. 45in (115cm) high ☆☆

Schuco

Schuco was founded as Schreyer and Co in Nuremberg, Germany and produced small mechanical tinplate toys. In 1921, the name Schuco was officially registered as a trademark. Along with bears, Schuco continued to produce vast numbers of clockwork toys.

"You really don't have to be young to find a friend in a teddy bear."

RACHEL NEWMAN

▲ *Three 1920s/30s miniature Schuco bears, in red, green and pink, each wearing knitted tunics. 3.5in (9cm) high* ☆☆ *each*

▲ *A very rare 1920s/30s Schuco miniature tumbling bear, with working wind-up mechanism. 5in (12.5cm) high* ✩✩✩

Schuco and vanity bears

The miniature bears for which Schuco is perhaps best known were first produced in 1924. They feature the same quality and attention to detail as the company's larger toys and tend to be similar to them in style. Initially designed as a publicity item and sales bonus give-away, these tiny bears, monkeys and mice became so popular that full production followed almost immediately.

The range includes novelty bears, which concealed perfume bottles, powder compacts and lipsticks or manicure sets, and a range of clockwork acrobatic and tumbling bears. These novelties are very collectable, particularly in rare colours such as orange and purple. They continued to be made until the 1970s.

◀ *A 1920s/30s Schuco miniature lavender-coloured manicure set bear, containing a Bakelite and metal nail buffer and file and a lipstick, with original 'Made in Germany' tag. This manicure set bear was made in several shades and this is one of the rarest colours.*
5in (12.5cm) high ☆☆☆☆

▶ A Schuco peach-
coloured mohair perfume
bottle bear, with pin back.
The head pulls off to reveal
a perfume bottle. 1930s
3.5in (9cm) high ☆☆☆

142

◀ *A 1920s/30s Schuco miniature yellow-gold perfume bottle bear. 5in (12.5cm) high* ☆☆☆

▶ A Schuco miniature bear in a 'Roller' vehicle, stamped on the side with the Schuco logo. In the 1930s Schuco introduced cars called Rollers for their miniature animals to ride. They were made of tinplate, and were driven by a friction movement. *c1930 5in (12.5cm) high* ☆☆☆

"Please don't feed the bears, they're stuffed already."
ANONYMOUS

▲ *A Schuco pink miniature bear, in a Roller vehicle. Unusual colours of mohair such as pink, purple and green command much higher prices. c1930 3.25in (8cm) high* ☆☆☆

◀ *A 1920s Schuco 'Yes-No' gold mohair plush bear. 18in (46cm) high ☆☆☆*

▶ *A Schuco 'Yes/No' bear, with working tail mechanism for nodding and shaking head. 1950s 5in (13cm) high ✩✩*

Schuco

Schreyer and Co., the company more commonly known as Schuco, was founded in Nuremberg, Germany in 1912 by Heinrich Schreyer, a furniture salesman, and Heinrich Müller, a previous employee at Gebrüder Bing (see page 173). The company produced small mechanical tinplate toys, including animals, walking soldiers, clowns and other figures, and was very successful until it was forced to close with the outbreak of World War I. When it reopened in 1918, Müller had a new partner, Adolph Kahn. Three years later, the name Schuco was officially registered as their trademark.

In 1921 Schuco introduced the 'Yes/No' bear, which was shown at the Leipzig Fair. This imaginative creation contained a metal rod inside the bear's body connecting a joint at the tail with a joint at the neck, so that waggling the tail produced nodding and shaking movements of the head. The Yes/No bears were produced in a range of sizes and with short, long, and extra-long plush fur. Diamanté eyes that sparkled in the light could also be fitted for an extra cost.

After a period producing telephone equipment for the war effort, Schuco restarted full production of toys at the end of the 1940s. In 1950 the Yes/No bear was reintroduced with an updated design – downturned paws, eyes wider apart, a more pronounced snout, and ears set higher on the head – and a new label marked 'Tricky'. The Tricky range was expanded to include pandas, chimpanzees and monkeys in 1953, and was made until 1960 when a new, soft stuffed range named 'Heiga' was introduced. During the 1960s and 70s fierce competition from the Far East was putting Schuco under pressure, and in 1976 the company was forced to sell out to toy manufacturer Dunbee Combex Marx.

◀ *A Schuco 'Yes/No' bear, with peach gold mohair, in excellent condition. 1950s 18in (46cm) high* ☆☆☆

> *"Bears sleep by day.*
> *At night they stay*
> *awake to chase*
> *away bad dreams."*

JESSIE O'NEIL

▶ A 1960s/70s Schuco footballer bear, the head of golden mohair, with 'pipe cleaner' body and limbs, in original dress that may have been associated with a German club. 3.75in (9.5cm) high ☆☆

◀ A Schuco miniature bear, with brown mohair and metal body, wearing a metal crown, with a green and yellow cord loop with BP button attached around the neck. This bear was given away as a promotional gift at BP petrol stations between 1958-1960. 3in (7.5cm) high ☆☆

Merrythought

One of the leading British soft toy manufacturers and still operating today, Merrythought is most famous for its recognisable 'Cheeky' bear. This cheerful fellow is still being produced in special editions each year (see pages 251–3). Most of the bears belonging to children born in Britain in the 1930s or 1960s would have been made by either Merrythought or Chad Valley.

▶ *A 1930s/40s Merrythought bear, with 'Hygienic Toys' label, in fairly good condition. 16in (40.5cm) high* ☆☆

◀ A 1930s/40s Merrythought bear with rare celluloid button on back. This design is often mistaken for a Chiltern bear. 23in (58.5cm) high ☆☆

Merrythought

Merrythought is a 17th century English word for wishbone and that symbol of good luck features on the buttons and labels of some of the quirky bears made by Merrythought.

The factory was established in 1930 at Coalbrookdale, near Ironbridge, Shropshire, by W.G. Holmes and H.G. Laxton. The two men had been partners since 1919, when they had opened a spinning mill to make mohair yarn, which they now decided to use in making teddy bears. C.J. Rendell, head of production at Chad Valley Toys, was lured away to work for Merrythought and he brought with him other skilled workers, including Florence Attwood, who was responsible for designing most Merrythought toys until 1949. It is not surprising, therefore, that many early Merrythought bears have features in common with Chad Valley bears. Other features, such as the webbed claw stitching, display the influence of J.K. Farnell, as Merrythought's sales director, A.C. Janisch, had previously worked for that company.

Popular designs include the dressed Bingie bears (produced 1931–8) and the 'Cheeky' bears, introduced in 1957 and still in production today. From 1954–80, various Disney characters, such as Lady and the Tramp, were produced and these are also very collectable.

The most famous individual Merrythought bear belonged to land and water speed record breaker Donald Campbell. Campbell, who refused to drive without his bear, Mr Whoppit, died during a record attempt on Coniston in 1967, while driving the jet hydroplane Bluebird K7. Merrythought re-issued a limited production of 5,000 replicas of Mr. Whoppit in the late 1990s.

◀ *A Merrythought bear, with long mohair plush and kapok and Excelsior stuffing, felt paw pads, four claws indicated by stitching with a connecting stitch across the base, stitched nose, amber and black glass eyes, celluloid ear button and fabric label to foot. 1930 24in (61cm) high* ☆☆☆

▶ *A Merrythought 'Punkinhead' bear, with brown mohair body and pale chest and ear linings, sewn-on velvet shorts, fully jointed, in good condition. With his white mohair topknot and black and white glass eyes, Punkinhead was a forerunner to the 'Cheeky' bear. 1951 14in (35.5cm) high* ☆☆☆☆

▲ A 1960s Merrythought 'Cheeky' bear, the golden mohair in
excellent condition, with label to foot. 10in (25.5cm) high ☆☆

Merrythought Cheeky bear

With its infectious smile and soft, kapok-filled body, Merrythought's 'Cheeky' bear has proved to be perennially popular. Designed by Jean Barber in 1956, the first Cheekys went on sale in 1957 and limited editions are still made today.

Cheeky bears have bells in their large, floppy ears, a beak-like velveteen muzzle and plastic safety eyes. Other identifying features include round felt paws and a large, circular head that looks too big for the body. The first Cheeky bears were made in gold mohair and a fine beige artificial silk plush, but by the 1960s examples were being made from an artificial sheepskin and a range of pastel colours and shades of gold and brown. Modern examples are made from mohair or acrylic. Most bears are jointed, but some have fixed limbs and a cotton fabric body which gives the appearance that the bear is wearing clothes.

The bear has proved so popular that Merrythought has designed many different models including a pyjama case and the bendable Mr and Mrs Twisty Cheeky, made from 1966-1988, which could be twisted into different poses. Cheekies are also highly collectable – in 2002 a rare open-mouthed bear sold for more than £2,000 at Christie's in London.

◀ *A Merrythought 'Cheeky' teddy bear, the large ears with bell sewn inside them, one foot labelled 'Merrythought Ironbridge Shropshire Made in England Regd. Design'. c1960 24in (61cm) high ☆☆*

▶ An early Merrythought 'Cheeky' bear, with art silk plush fur and stuffed with kapok, with bells in ears, no label. c1960
12in (30.5cm) high ☆☆

▲ *A Merrythought 'Mr Twisty Cheeky' bear. Mr Twisty Cheeky has an internal wire so that he can be twisted into different poses. There was also a Mrs Twisty Cheeky made, wearing a matching outfit with a skirt. 1966–68 11in (28cm) high* ☆☆

▶ *A 1970s Merrythought bear, with plastic eyes, label on the right foot. 10in (25.5cm) high* ☆

"A teddy's heart is as big as his smile."

ANONYMOUS

▶ *A modern Merrythought 'Curly Gold' bear, fully jointed, with curly gold mohair. Merrythought's classic bears remain little changed since the 1950s. 18in (46cm) high* ☆

▶ *A Merrythought large teddy bear. c2000 20in (51cm) high.* ☆

◀ *A 1990s Merrythought bear, with leather paw pads and original labels, in mint condition. 14in (35.5cm) high* ☆

Other Makers

From the beginning of the twentieth century, when bear production first got underway, there has been a firm place in our hearts for the teddy bear. Many makers have sought to produce the most loveable bears: at the height of teddy bear manufacturing in Germany there were over 270 different bear factories. Bears have also played their part in our culture, with some of our best-loved fictional characters being furry teddy friends.

"There is a personal relationship with teddy bears that never releases its grip. Who can forget perhaps the only friend who really understood?"

BARBARA WERKMASTER, EVA-LENA BENGSSTON AND PER PETERSON

▲ *A 1950s Austrian Berg teddy bear, with heart and red ribbon. 5.5in (14cm) high* ☆

◀ An Austrian 1950s/60s Berg bear, with an enamel heart tag to chest printed 'BERG' to reverse. 5.5in (14cm) high ☆

Bing

Gebrüder Bing was founded in Nuremberg by Ignaz and Adolf Bing in 1865 and became famous for its mechanical toys. Bing first began to make bears in 1907 but their design quickly became a source of conflict with Steiff, who started legal action against them for the use of a metal arrow in the bears' ears. Steiff considered the metal tag to be too similar to their trademark button-in-the-ear, and Bing was eventually forced to replace it with a metal label in 1920.

Though Bing bears typically have very appealing faces and are greatly sought after, the company is particularly famous for their mechanical bears. The first mechanical bear was made in 1908, and contained a clockwork mechanism that allowed the head to move from side to side. Pull-along bears on wheels, some large enough for a child to ride, were also popular. The somersaulting bear was introduced in 1910, prompting further disagreement with Steiff who claimed it to be a copy of their 'Purzel Bear' (1909). Further legal action followed that only ended in 1915 when Bing stopped production of the somersaulting bear.

In the 1920s Bing sought to distance itself from Steiff by introducing changes to their designs. While early Bing bears had been similar in style to those of their rival, the snout now became longer with distinctive stitching and a wide smile. The bear was successful and produced in a range of sizes.

In 1927 the company's president, Stephan Bing, resigned as a result of discrimination against Jewish firms under Hitler's Nazi regime. The company struggled on under new management, but eventually closed in 1932.

◄ *An early 20thC German bear, possibly Bing, of top-quality mohair, in excellent condition, with deep boot button eyes, tag missing. c1910 21in (53cm) high* ☆☆☆☆

"You have only to look at a genuine teddy's face to see at once the loyalty, common sense, and above all, dependability behind it."

PETER BULL

◀ *A small Bing clockwork football-playing teddy bear. c1910 8in (20.5cm) high* ☆☆☆

▲ *A Bing bear, with golden mohair, and vertically stitched nose. All of the larger Bing bears, from 16in (41cm) upwards, have vertically stitched noses, while the smaller bears have horizontally stitched noses. c1925 16in (41cm) high* ☆☆☆☆

"All bears merit a Dignified Old Age."

PETER GRAY

▶ *A Character Toy Co. teddy bear, with felt pads, and remnants of a label. The larger pads and paws and heavier limbs show a transition from the long narrow body typical of early American bears, to a shorter, more rounded design. c1940 14in (35.5cm) high* ☆

▲ *A German long gold mohair plush bear, with felt paw pads, shaved muzzle, and growler. c1950 19in (48cm) high* ☆☆

Dean's

Dean's Rag Book Company was founded in 1903 by Henry Samuel Dean to launch his brightly coloured, printed rag books for children who 'wear their food and eat their clothes'. The first Dean's teddy bears, called the 'Kuddlemee' range, were not made until 1915 and large-scale production of teddy bears only followed in the 1920s.

The 1930s was Dean's most productive period. In 1931, art silk was used create 'Silkeen Teddy', available in two sizes and assorted colours. By 1932 art silk had replaced mohair, which wasn't used again until 1937. The distinctive 'mouse-eared' bears, with round heads and ears set on the side of the head, were also launched in the 1930s and were produced into the 1950s, despite the difficulty of continuing during World War II when business almost ceased.

Lock-in safety eyes were introduced in the 1950s after Dean's had made a partial recovery and by the 1960s Dean's had embarked on a safety campaign, making all of their bears suitable for children.

When London Zoo's first polar bear to be born in captivity, Brumas, arrived in 1949, Dean's produced a mohair version of the mother polar bear, Ivy, holding her new cub. Other teddies based on real bears followed, created by Dean's designer, Sylvia Willgoss, in the 1950s and 1970s.

The company went into liquidation in 1988, but former employee, Neil Miller organized a management buy-out and now runs Dean's as Managing Director. Dean's Collector's Club, launched in 1994, claims to be one of the biggest teddy bear clubs in the world, and aims to recreate Dean's early bears, with all their traditional characteristics, for members to collect.

◀ *A probably Dean's Rag Book magenta mohair bear, with velvet pads and blue glass eyes. c1930 18in (45.5cm) high* ☆☆☆

▶ *A Dean's Rag Book Co. blue bear, with round head and cupped ears. c1926*
18in (45.5cm) high
☆☆

▲ *A Dean's Rag book gold mohair bear with shaved snout. c1930s 18in (45cm) high* ☆☆

▲ *A 1950s German Diem beige teddy bear, with short plush fur, stitched snout, glass eyes, a swivel-jointed body, and a growler. The feet are noticeably bigger than those on earlier bears, and the arms slightly curved, not straight. 19in (48cm) high* ☆☆

"A Teddy bear will always care. When all else fails hug your teddy."
ANONYMOUS

◀ *A 1950s German Diem gold mohair bear. 15.5in (39.5cm) high* ✩✩

▲ *A 1950s German Diem bear, yellow mohair fur to body and short plush mohair on snout and paws, with growler. Diem was a German maker who used high quality materials. 24in (61cm) high* ☆☆

"Everything in life I share, except of course my teddy bear."

ANONYMOUS

▲ *An English teddy bear, possibly Dean's, with glass eyes and gold mohair plush and jointed limbs, some wear. c1930s 28in (71cm) high ☆☆*

The tag reads: "To LONDON. Via. PADDINGTON. STATION."

Paddington

Paddington Bear was found by Mr and Mrs Brown at Paddington station, sitting on a suitcase, wearing nothing but a hat and a label around his neck that read, 'Please Look After This Bear. Thank You.' It transpired that he had been sent to England from Darkest Peru by his Aunt Lucy, now in a home for retired bears, and that he had survived the crossing by eating marmalade.

Thus begins Michael Bond's much-loved series of children's stories. Inspired by a bear he gave his wife as a Christmas present in 1956 (also named Paddington), Bond wrote his first book in ten days. 'A Bear Called Paddington' was published two years later in 1958. Since then the Paddington books have been translated into over thirty languages, Bond has penned television and film scripts for his bear, and large amounts of Paddington merchandize has been produced to keep up with the incredible demand.

The first toy Paddington was created in 1972 by Shirley and Eddie Clarkson of Gabrielle Designs, the prototype made as a Christmas present for their children Joanna and Jeremy (future presenter of British television programme 'Top Gear'). This Paddington was dressed in Wellington boots to help him stand upright. Initially these were small children's boots manufactured by Dunlop, but when demand became too great, Gabrielle Designs began producing its own boots, with paw prints moulded into the soles. It held the world exclusive rights to Paddington Bear until 1976, but now supplies solely to Britain. American Paddingtons have been produced by Eden Toys from 1975.

◀ *A British Gabrielle Designs 'Paddington' teddy bear, by Shirley Clarkson, with hat, duffel coat, Wellingtons and luggage tag. 1972 18in (46cm) high* ☆

▶ *A Gabrielle Designs 'Aunt Lucy' bear, complete with clothing and accessories, including Peruvian coins in a pocket in her petticoats. Aunt Lucy is much harder to find than Paddington. c1970 18in (46cm) high ☆☆*

▲ *A 1960s German Grisly bear, with synthetic plush fur, and button to chest. 14in (35.5cm) high* ☆

▶ *A British Harwin & Co. 'Old Mac' bear, from the Guy Campbell Collection, wearing a part-recreated uniform. c1914-18 16in (40.5cm) high* ☆☆☆

▶ *A German Rudolf Haas 'Nickle Knackle' bear, with a mechanism inside that makes the bear's head nod when his left arm is moved and shake when his right arm is moved. c1930s 16in (40.5cm) high* ☆☆☆

Hermann

Based between the Thuringian Forest and the city of Sonneberg, the world centre of toy production of the day, it was little wonder that Johann Hermann made a living carving toys from Thuringian wood. But he can hardly have thought, when he began his business around 1907, that it would grow into the huge Hermann teddy bear dynasty that exists today.

Three of his children, Max, Arthur and Adelheid, set up a teddy bear company in 1913 trading under the name Johann Hermann Toy Factory. In 1920 Max moved to set up his own company and quickly established himself as an important name in bear manufacturing. At the beginning of the 1930s he created his now-famous green triangle logo, and the company he started is still active today, under the name Hermann-Spielwaren GmbH.

A second company, also making teddy bears, was set up by Johann's eldest son, Bernhard. Bernhard's sons Hellmut, Artur and Werner continued the company after their father's death in 1959, having changed the name in 1952 from Bernhard Hermann to Gebrüder Hermann. This company is also still operating today. Both firms continue to be recognized for their quality bears.

◀ *A 1930s Hermann bear, pin jointed. 6.75in (17cm) high* ☆☆

> *"A teddy bear does not depend upon mechanics to give him the semblance of life. He is loved, and therefore he lives."*
>
> PAM BROWN

▲ *A 1950s German Bernhard Hermann 'Zotty' type teddy bear, with original ribbon and bell, in good condition. 14in (35.5cm) high ☆☆*

▲ *A 1950s Australian Joy Toys gold mohair bear with label on foot. 14in (35.5cm) high* ☆☆

Knickerbocker

Taking its name from the baggy knickerbockers trousers worn by the Dutch settlers in New York, the Knickerbocker Toy Company was founded in Albany, New York in 1869. Initially it produced educational toys, such as alphabet blocks. The first teddy bears can be dated to the 1920s, when the company introduced permanent labels on its toys.

Knickerbocker bears can be identified not only by their labels, but also by their separately sewn-in muzzles, very wide heads, short snouts, big cupped ears, and paw pads of velveteen. Early bears were predominantly made of gold, brown, or white mohair. Some have metal noses, while others have the more conventional stitched nose that became standard in Knickerbocker bears after the 1930s.

From 1968–77, Knickerbocker was licensed to produce Smokey Bear for the American Forest Fire Prevention Campaign. Named after Smokey Joe Martin, a famous New York fire-fighter, Smokey was introduced in 1944 and is typically seen wearing denim trousers, a belt buckle, badge and a yellow hat. Knickerbocker's Smokey became very popular and many were produced, including a talking version, with a built-in tape that reminded his owners how to prevent forest fires.

The company moved to new premises in Middlesex, New Jersey in 1960s and continued to produce cheerful, large-eared bears until 1984, when Knickerbocker went bankrupt and ceased trading.

A family named Knickerbocker began trading as the Knickerbocker Bear Company in 1990, but these bears are unrelated.

◀ *A 1940s Knickerbocker cinnamon bear, with glass eyes and velveteen pads, the round ears set characteristically low down on the head, the shape of the head and thin snout are also typical of this maker. c1935 16.25in (41cm) high* ☆☆

▲ A 1930s German Moritz Pappe musical bear, containing a musical mechanism. 17in (43cm) high ☆☆☆

▶ A 1930s German musical bear, containing a Helvetic mechanism, with dual tipped pale gold and vivid yellow mohair. 18in (45.5cm) high ☆☆

"Baths may be lovely for people, but bears are not that keen. When did you last see or har of a bear taking a bath, willingly?"

TED MENTION

▶ *A 1920s very large Omega bear. 24in (61cm) high* ☆☆☆☆

◀ A British
Omega blonde
mohair bear.
1920s 24in
(61cm) high
☆☆☆☆

> *"Why do I leave the zip of my bag a little open? So that bear can breathe, of course."*

PATRICIA HITCHCOCK

▲ *A British Omega bear, with upward-curving snout. c1920 14.5in (37cm) high* ☆☆☆

▲ *A c1930 Peacock & Sons teddy bear, with angular head, chunky arms and arched, square snout, heavy black stitching, Peacock label on right foot. 28in (71cm) high* ☆☆☆☆

▲ *A 1950s English Pedigree bear, in pink and white mohair. This is an unusual colour for this maker. 14in (35.5cm) high* ☆☆

▲ A Pedigree bear, with jointed limbs and fixed head, and bells in the ears. The design is similar to Merrythought's 'Cheeky'. c1960 14in (35.5cm) high ✩✩

▶ A 1930s French Pintel bright yellow mohair plush teddy, with boot button eyes and pin joints. 6.5in (16.5cm) high ✩✩

"Age simply doesn't enter into it! The older the friend, the more he is valued."

PETER BULL

"One never quite gets over a lost bear."

JANE SWAN

▲ *A 1940s English Pixie Toys bear, with tag. Pixe bears typically have webbed stitching on their paws.* ☆☆

◀ *A German Strunz tumbling mechanical bear, with damaged mechanism. c1912 10in (25.5cm) high ☆☆*

◀ *An Irish Tara Toys bear, in mint condition, the mouth opening mechanism operated by levers at the back of the head. 1950s 14in (35.5cm) high* ☆☆

> *"All you have between you and 'The Dark' is bear."*
>
> HELEN THOMSON

▲ *A pre-World War I English bear, possibly by Terry's, with repairs and restorations. 18in (45.5cm) high* ☆☆

◀ *A mid-20thC English bear, possibly made by Terry's, with metal joints outside body. 16.5in (42cm) high* ☆☆☆

▲ *A 1940s/50s Belgian Unica pink bear, made of art silk. 14in (35.5cm) high* ☆☆

"What is it about this inanimate object of fur and stuffing that makes it so hard to part with?"

SARAH MCCLENNAN

▶ *A German 1930s/40s Weiersmüller bear. 16in (40.5cm) high* ☆☆

◀ *A 1950s American mascot bear, for the University of California. 16in (40.5cm) high* ☆

Wendy Boston

When Wendy Boston's husband, Ken Williams, returned from the Second World War to their home in Crickhowell, South Wales, he found his wife had spent the War years making various soft toys in the limited range of fabrics available. As there had been few toys manufactured during the war, these teddies were much appreciated by family and friends so Williams founded a company and began selling them to local businesses, with great success. As Boston continued to design the toys, Williams continued to market them, and by 1948 they had to move to a larger factory, in nearby Abergavenny.

Wendy Boston's unique selling point was that her toys were 'Play Safe'. They were made of washable synthetic fabrics, and had screw-in eyes that did not contain glass or wire. The first fully washable, un-jointed bear was developed in 1954. A year later the washable bear was launched, washed and put through a mangle on British television, a marketing ploy that proved a great success.

By 1964 Wendy Boston Playsafe Toys Ltd produced over 25 per cent of UK soft toy exports. But growing competition with cheap imports from the Far East combined with the added cost of producing the safety features caused company profits to fall. In 1968, the company was taken over by Denys Fisher Toys, who continued to produce soft toys using the Wendy Boston name until 1976.

◀ *An English Wendy Boston bear, unjointed, with glass eyes, the fur a gold mohair mix. c1960 16in (40.5cm) high* ☆

▲ *An American Woolnough gold mohair Pooh Bear, with foot stamp. c1930 14in (35.5cm) high* ☆☆☆☆☆

▶ *An English blonde mohair miniature bear, in much-loved condition. c1914 5.5in (14cm) high* ☆☆

"The appeal of a teddy bear is universal and to all ages."

MARGARET HUTCHINGS

◀ *A rare pre-World War I purse bear, by an unknown maker. 16in (40.5cm) long* ☆☆

▲ *A pre-World War I English gold mohair bear, with an unusual face and plump shape. 13.5in (34cm) high* ☆☆

"Teddy bears are so versatile; they can be companions, playthings, bedfellows... Goodness, what other creatures can play so many varied roles?!"

VICTORIA MARSDEN

▲ *A pair of 1920s English bears, possibly made on special order as a pair. Tallest 21.5in (54.5cm) high* ☆☆☆

◀ *A 1920s English bear, by an unknown maker. 24in (61cm) high*
☆☆☆

▲ *A large 1920s/30s German bear, in dark pink dual-tipped mohair, with hump, stuffed with wood wool. 34in (86cm) high* ☆☆☆

"Teddy might be
full of stuffing,
but he always
holds onto his
moral sense,
even when there
is dreadful
(usually edible)
temptation."

JOSA KEYES

◀ *A 1930s French Faye silk
plush teddy, with metal joints.
6.5in (16.5cm) high* ☆☆

▶ *A cotton plush bear, in orange, yellow and pale gold mohair, containing wooden mechanism that opens the mouth when the is tummy is squeezed. c1930 14in (35.5cm) high*
☆☆

▲ *A 1930s German golden mohair musical bear, by an unknown maker. Squeezing his body activates the musical mechanism. 15in (38cm) high* ☆☆

▲ *A 1930s American amethyst-coloured mohair plush bear, with unusual square shoulders and upturned paws, glass eyes and velvet pads. 24in (61cm) high* ☆☆

▲ *A 1930s English blonde mohair bear, by an unidentified maker. 14in (35.5cm) high* ☆☆

◀ *A 1930s probably English bear, with Rexine pads and glass eyes, in good condition. c1940 14in (35.5cm) high* ☆☆

▲ *A late 1930s brown-tipped blonde mohair bear. 13.75in (35cm) high* ☆☆

"Please look after this bear."

MICHAEL BOND

▲ *An Eastern Europen cotton plush bear,*
with pin joints. c1950 8in (20.5cm) high ☆☆

▲ *A 1950s gold mohair English teddy bear. 16in (40.5cm) high* ☆☆

▶ *A 1950s Continental bear, made of cotton plush, with growler and repairs. 18in (45.5cm) high* ☆

◀ *A 1930s German lavender-coloured bear. 23in (58.5cm)* ☆☆

Limited
Editions

These collectors' bears are typically made in limited runs of up to 500. The fewer examples in the edition, the more the bears are likely to keep or grow in value in the long term. Such bears should be kept with their box and other packaging and all relevant paperwork.

"Only the best is good enough for our children."

MARGARETE STEIFF

▲ *A Steiff '1908 Rosé Replica' bear, from an edition of 3,000, in box with certificate. In 1908 Steiff produced samples in black, pink, green and yellow mohair for the English market. This is a replica of the pink sample bear. 2008 13.75in (35cm) high* ☆☆

▶ *A limited edition Steiff 'Vintage 1908 Replica' bear, with 'wear' patches and holes to felt paws, with black glass eyes and growler, in presentation box, from an edition of 1,908. c2009 12.5in (32cm) high* ☆☆

Karl Lagerfeld bear

Karl Lagerfeld, the famous fashion designer, doesn't remember having a teddy bear as a child. 'I never played with anything like toys', he said, 'I wanted to be grown-up'. However, when invited by Steiff to collaborate on a limited edition Karl Lagerfeld bear that was released in 2008, he accepted.

No expense was spared in making Lagerfeld's furry lookalike, from the quality white alpaca fur and the white gold ear button, to the Swarowski crystal attached to a black silk cravat. The materials for the clothes, including Italian wool for the jacket, leather for the belt and lacquered denim for the jeans, were individually selected and made in Lagerfeld's Paris Studio.

The bear's haughty expression is endearingly at odds with traditional Steiff faces, but manages to capture the essence of the man himself. Naturally, his eyes are masked by impenetrable dark sunglasses, which were taken from the 'Lagerfeld eyewear' line.

The bear's production run was limited to 2,500 pieces worldwide, with each bear having a special woven white and red ear tag and a unique number. However, Lagerfeld's identity is not quite as exclusive as the bear might make it seem, as he has already been immortalized in a video game, and as a plastic toy.

◀ *A limited edition Steiff 'Karl Lagerfeld' bear, designed by German fashion designer Karl Lagerfeld, with exclusive white gold button and tag in ear, from an edition of 2,500, in presentation box with certificate. 2008 15.5cm (40cm) high ☆☆☆*

◀ *A Steiff 'Classic 1909' teddy bear, yellow label and gold-plated button-in-ear. c2009 13.75in (35cm) high* ☆☆

▶ *A Steiff 'Xenia' limited edition bear, in off-white aged mohair, with loose joints, growler, silk ribbon bow and portrait brooch of Alfonzo in gold-plated frame, from an edition of 1,500, in presentation box. Xenia is named after Princess Xenia Georgievna of Russia who owned the famous Steiff teddy bear 'Alfonzo' (see page 22–3). 2008 17.75in (43cm) high* ☆☆

When everyone else has let you down, there's always Ted.

CLARA ORTEGA

▲ *A limited edition Steiff 'George' bear, of gold mohair with felt paws, pale amber and black glass eyes, filled with wood wool, from an edition of 2,000, in presentation felt bag. c2009 12in (30cm) high* ☆☆

▶ *A Steiff limited edition*
'Henderson' bear, of long
curled mohair, with a
growler in the body,
from an edition of 2,000,
in presentation box.
The bear is named
after Colonel Bob
Henderson (see page
69). c2009 21.5in
(55cm) high ☆☆

Rupert Bear

Rupert Bear, a human-like bear in red jumper, checked trousers and scarf, made his first appearance in 1920. Living with his parents in Nutwood, Rupert usually starts out on a small errand for his mother or on a visit to one of his 'chums' and finds himself on a strange and wonderful adventure.

He was created by English artist Mary Tourtel for the *Daily Express* as a rival to the *Daily Mail*'s cartoon character, Teddy Tail, and was followed by Pip, Squeak and Wilfred in the *Daily Mirror*, all of whom are now forgotten. Not so Rupert, who became popular almost immediately. In 1935 when Tourtel retired artist Alfred Bestall took over the illustration of the *Daily Express* Rupert stories, and improved their plots. Despite the paper shortage that kept all the other newspaper characters from making appearances, Rupert comics continued throughout World War II, as it was felt that his disappearance would damage morale.

After the War, the comic strips were translated into many languages and books and annuals followed. Soft toy versions of Rupert were not made until the 1960s, by Merrythought and Pedigree Toys in Britain, and Real Soft Toys in the USA.

Rupert has appeared in three television series (the first featuring Rupert as a puppet) and in 1984 he featured in a short animated film, 'Rupert and the Frog Song', written by Paul McCartney and including the song 'We All Stand Together'.

◀ *A Steiff 'Rupert Bear', with dense white alpaca fur, wearing traditional Rupert outfit, with stitch-sculpted fingers and thumb to hands like the original character, in presentation box with certificate, from limited edition of 3,000. c2009 11in (28cm) high* ☆☆

▶ *A Steiff limited edition 'Georgina Guardian Angel Bear', of wavy pale blue mohair with white mohair wings, wearing a sterling silver 'G' pendant, white felt paws, button and tag in ear, from an edition of 1,500. 2003 9.75in (25cm) high* ☆☆

▲ *A limited edition Merrythought 'Billy' bear, inspired by an original Farnell bear, of wavy beige mohair, with velveteen paws with blanket-stitched claws, glass eyes, stuffed with polyfibre and plastic pellets for weight and wood shavings in his muzzle, with presentation certificate, from an edition of 200. c2009 20in (51cm) high ☆☆*

◄ A limited edition
Merrythought 'Little
Patchwork Punkie' bear,
with 23 patches in
different coloured mohair,
felt paws and glass eyes,
from an edition of 150.
c2009 8in (20cm) high ☆

"I am a Bear of Very Little Brain and long words bother me."

WINNIE-THE-POOH

▲ *A limited edition Merrythought bear, 'Happy Cheeky'. 2009 25.25in (38cm) high* ☆☆

◀ *A limited edition*
Merrythought
'Cheeky Toggles'
bear. 2009 11.5in
(29cm) high ☆☆

> *"Bears being sent through the mail should never be squashed up to make them fit. It gives them indigestion."*
>
> PAM BROWN

▶ *A limited edition Merrythought 'Sleepy Cheeky' bear. 2009 25.25in (38cm) high ✩✩*

Artist bears

Bear artists design and make short, limited editions of some of the most appealing and unusual bears on the market today. Each example shows the remarkable imagination, skill and creativity of the artist. The first artist bears were made on the West Coast of America in the 1970s, but their popularity ensured they were soon being made all over the world. The selection that follows shows a small number of the artist bears available today.

◀ *A British artist bear, 'Brennus', by Jean and Bill Ashburner, with a needle-sculpted nose and realistic three-dimensional paw pads, from a limited edition of 8. 'Brennus' means 'king' or 'prince' in Latin and Celtic. c2009 18in (46cm) high* ☆☆

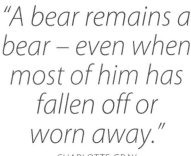

"A bear remains a bear – even when most of him has fallen off or worn away."

CHARLOTTE GRAY

◀ *An American artist bear, 'Little Winnie Winky', by Jody Battaglia, made of aged brass-coloured mohair, wearing cotton bloomers under her polka dot skirt, with squeaker, filled with wood shavings and fully jointed, from a limited edition of 10. Jody Battaglia, from Georgia, takes inspiration from illustrations in old children's books and has made bears since 1979. c2009 8in (20cm) high ☆☆*

Aline Cousin

While visiting a second-hand market in her home town in the suburbs of Paris in 1990, Aline Cousin fell in love with a Steiff polar bear, only to find the bear was no longer for sale! It was this disappointment that inspired her to make her own bears.

It took her two months to collect her materials, as there seemed to be no specialized shops selling mohair or glass eyes. As she had no experience in making teddy bears, Cousin bought herself a tatty 1960s bear, with his cardboard joints showing through, to examine his proportions. She also studied photographs of old bears and her own childhood toys, Nounours no. 1 and Nounours no. 2, both of whom still live in her bedroom. The first bear attempt was difficult, his arms and body were too long and thin, he didn't have a hump, and she remade the head several times. She finally created her first bear, Théodore, after two months' hard work.

To the surprise of friends and family, Cousin's passion for bear-making grew, and she continued to make bears in all kinds of fabrics and sizes. In April 1991, during a search for glass eyes, Cousin met Valerie Loiret who invited her to present her bears at the newly created 'le Club français de l'ours ancien' – the next day! Cousin worked through the night to make her bears as attractive as possible and received great acclaim and encouragement from the new society.

Since then, Cousin has witnessed a huge increase in popularity of bear-making in France, and has made many more bears, including 'Berlington', who was created for the Louvre in Paris and now resides in the Musée des Arts Décoratifs.

◀ *An artist bear, 'Boulton', by Aline Cousin, no. 2 of 15. c2009 5.5 in (13.5cm) high* ☆

◀ *A New Zealand artist bear, 'Montgomery Merrieweather', by Joan Easton, made of sparse blonde mohair, wearing a silk clown suit and matching hat, no. 6 from an edition of 8. 2008 6.25in (16cm) high* ☆☆

▲ *A unique Canadian artist bear, 'Hugo Babbit', by Forget-me-Not Bears. 2009 7.5in (20cm) high* ☆☆

▲ *A unique Canadian artist bear, by Forget-me-Not Bears. 2009 16in (40.5cm) high* ☆☆

▲ *A Japanese artist bear, 'Nichiz2', by Miyuki Fukushima, with Indian glass bead eyes and sequined wool scarf. c2009 10in (25cm) high* ☆☆

▶ *A large American artist bear, 'Johnnie Witherspoon', by Mary George, of honey-gold mohair with black glass eyes and felt paws, from a limited edition of 8. c2009 26in (66cm) high*
☆☆

"Remember when I said teddy can't sleep without me? Well, truth is, I can't sleep without teddy."

WEBSTER PAPADOPOLIS

▲ *An American artist bear, 'Harrison' by Mary George, with curly pale cinnamon mohair on a brown backing, from a limited edition of 10. c2009 13in (33cm) high* ☆☆

"If you go down to the woods today, you're sure of a big surprise..."

JIMMY KENNEDY

◀ A Danish artist bear, 'Anton', by Yvonne Graubaek, with glass eyes and filled with pellets for added weight. c2009 9.5in (25.5cm) high ☆☆

▲ A Danish artist bear, 'Bastian', by Yvonne Graubaek, with brown alpaca fur, and leather thread claws and leather fore pads, from a limited edition of 8. c2009 14.5in (37cm) high ☆☆

"Exit, pursued by a bear."

WILLIAM SHAKESPEARE

▲ *A unique Australian artist bear, 'Rosebud Collectors' by Loris Hancock, with a miniature bear riding a bear on all fours. c2000 5in (12.5cm) high* ☆☆

▲ *A unique Australian artist bear, 'Swamp Dwellers' by Loris Hancock, the miniature bear riding a leaping frog. 2004* ☆☆

"Bears need people. People need bears."

PAM BROWN

▲ *A German Freche Früchte Bären (Cheeky Fruit Bears) artist bear, by Kerstin Jeske, the miniature bear sitting within flowers and leaves of felt. c2000 4in (10cm) high* ☆☆

◀ *A German Freche Früchte Bären 'cake' artist bear, by Kerstin Jeske, with label at the back in seam. c2000 4.75in (12cm) high* ☆

▶ *A German Freche*
Früchte Bären 'banana'
artist bear, by Kerstin Jeske,
with label at the back in
seam. c2000
2.5in (6cm) high ☆

▶ *A German Freche Früchte Bären 'blackberry' artist bear, by Kerstin Jeske, with label at the back in seam. c2000 4.75in (12cm) high* ☆

Hisa Kato

Japanese artist Hisa Kato has made bears and other soft sculptures since 1995. Her unconventional and challenging work has considerably influenced other artists in the US and Europe as well as Japan. 'Just do what you love,' Kato says, 'and the rest will follow.'

This philosophy certainly seems to have worked for Kato. When she made her first bear, she knew very little about teddy bears: 'I didn't know what a paper pattern was, so I proceeded to draw my design directly onto the yellow felt fabric.'

Now it is her originality, meticulous craftsmanship, innovative use of traditional materials, that sets Kato's bears apart. She starts from scratch each time, spending 'hours sculpting the nose, or several days to dye and treat the fabric to achieve the desired look. In fact,' she says, 'I spend so much time working on each bear that I have a special connection with every one of them.'

Her one-of-a-kind teddies range from tiny bears of 2in (5cm) high to giants of 31in (79cm) high. Kato draws her inspiration from reading children's picture books and observations from daily life.

In 1995 Kato exhibited her teddy bears for the first time at an art gallery and entered and won the Japan Teddy Bear Association contest. Since then she has exhibited her bears at shows and several art galleries with continued success.

◀ *A Japanese artist bear, 'Butterfly Sooty', by Hisa Kato, of gold mohair with black mohair ears and glass eyes, and moulded gypsum nose and butterfly wings, from a limited edition of 7. c2000 4.25in (11cm) high* ☆☆

"Look for the bare necessities, the simple bare necessities."

BALOO FROM *THE JUNGLE BOOK*

▲ *A British artist bear, 'Gabriel Oak', by June Kendall, with gold mohair and glass eyes, wearing a green-checked scarf, part filled with steel shot for weight, no. 6 of 12. June Kendall is based in Hampshire, and was inspired to make bears during Dorset's celebrations for the 150th anniversary of Thomas Hardy, and as a result named her creations 'Hardy Bears'. This bear is themed on Thomas Hardy's character in 'Far From the Madding Crowd'. 2008 4.25in (11cm) high* ☆

◀ An American artist bear, 'Stella', by Sue Lain, made with dusky pink mohair wearing a vintage broderie anglaise dress, no. 4 from an edition of 8. 2008 12in (30cm) high ☆☆

"A teddy bear in the hand is worth ten in the shop."

ANONYMOUS

▲ *A British artist bear, 'Miranda', by Elizabeth Leggat, made from antique short pile plush mohair, and wearing a 1920s-style silk dress trimmed with vintage ribbon, from a limited edition of 6. Miranda's bag is made from pieces of an original Edwardian purse. 2008 4in (10cm) high* ☆☆

▲ *An English miniature artist bear, 'Valentina', by Elisabeth Marsden, with knitted pink top and doll. c2009 2.75in (7cm) high* ☆

▲ *A pair of English miniature artist bears, 'Danny' and 'Maisie', by Elisabeth Marsden, wearing school uniform. c2009 2.75in (7cm) high* ☆ ☆

▲ *An English miniature artist bear, 'Mikey', by Elisabeth Marsden, with embroidered amd knitted jacket, split pin joints and glass eyes. c2009 2.75in (7cm) high* ☆

▶ *An English miniature artist bear, 'Buzby', by Elisabeth Marsden, with split pin joints and glass eyes. c2009 2.75in (7cm) high* ☆

◀ A German artist bear, 'Victor', by Daniela-Rebekka Melse, with long claws and felt pads, filled softly with wood shavings to give a floppy, 'loved' feel, from a limited edition of 8. 18in (45.5cm) high c2009 ☆☆

"Anyone who has looked a teddy bear in the face will recognize the friendly twinkle in his knowing look."

HAROLD NADOLNY

▲ A British artist bear, 'Dougal', by Wendy and Alan Mullaney, made of long pile fawn mohair on a pale brown backing cloth, with black glass eyes, and stuffed with wood wool, no. 4 from an edition of 6. c2009 19in (48cm) high ✩✩

◀ *A British artist bear, 'Black Prince' by Wendy and Alan Mullaney, made of distressed long pile black mohair, with amber and black glass eyes, and growler in body, no. 5 from an edition of 6.*
c2009 20in (51cm) high ☆☆

◀ *A Dutch artist bear, 'Benny', by Anjo Noija, with black shoe button eyes and loose threads that give the impression of wear, dressed in hand-knitted blue dungarees, no. 5 from an edition of 8. 2008 7.5in (19cm) high* ☆☆

▲ *A British artist bear, 'Lily's Playtime', by Micha Parnell, with blue glass eyes, crocheted hair ribbon, German spinning wooden top toy and fully-jointed 2in (5cm) cashmere bear, from a limited edition of 6. Micha Parnell, now living in Cornwall, grew up in Germany surrounded by Steiff toys and started making bears professionally in 1991. 2008 5.5in (14cm) high* ☆☆

Marie Robischon

Marie Robischon, from Freiburg, Germany, was interested in the craft of bear-making as a child, when she used scraps of old material to make teddy bears for her doll's house. After some years working as a graphic designer, she returned to bear making as a profession in the late 1980s.

Interested in the long tradition of the teddy bear, she works with the classical proportions of early German bears. To create an aged feel Robischon uses gently distressed mohair for the fur and vintage fabrics to make the bears' clothes. The stuffing is used to further enhance the effect of age, with deliberate understuffing at joints such as the elbows to create softness.

Notable for her beautiful combinations of fabrics, colours and textures, Robischon creates exceptionally detailed designs for the bears' clothes and often finishes off her creations with vintage accessories that are individual to each bear.

Robischon describes the creative process as 'like a good talk with friends. The real art is in the listening … You choose the words carefully – just like you choose the material of which a really good bear is made – but only when you hear the answer will you know whether you have 'said' the right thing.'

◀ *A German artist schoolboy bear, 'Rudi', by Marie Robischon, with sparse curly blonde mohair on brown backing cloth, dressed in a cotton shirt printed with letters of the alphabet, striped trousers, and a patchwork coat, comes with a bundle of vintage books, from a limited edition of 4. c2009 20in (50cm) high* ☆☆☆☆

▶ A German artist bear, 'Charlie', by Marie Robischon, made from vintage fabrics, from a limited edition. c2009 18.25in (46.5cm) high ☆☆☆☆

"Smarter than the average bear!"

YOGI BEAR

▲ *An American artist bear, 'Banjo', by Art Rogers, with painted felt nose and sculpted paws, from a limited edition of 8. 2008 10in (25cm) high* ☆☆

▲ *A German artist bear, 'Crazy Flat Bear',*
by Heidi Schaefer, made of green and
white mohair and painted around the
eyes and cheeks, wearing a silk ribbon
head band and a pearl necklace, no. 4 of
an edition of 8. 2008 7.25in (18cm) high ☆

▶ *A German artist bear, 'Lilly Belle*
Queen of Childhood', by Heidi Schaefer,
with 'roly poly' body, wearing velvet dress
and crown and carrying small teddy
bear, no. 3 of an edition of 8. 2004
8in (20cm) high ☆☆

▶ *A British artist bear, 'Sailor's Hope' by Jennie Sharman-Cox, with airbrushed detail to face, ears and paws, no. 4 of 8. This bear was inspired by a picture in a vintage advert of a girl waiting for her sailor. 2008 12in (30cm) high* ☆☆

"A bear, however hard he tries, goes tubby without exercise."

WINNIE-THE-POOH

▲ *An American artist bear, 'Algernon', by Jeanette Warner, made of sparse cinnamon mohair with black glass bead eyes and aged felt paws, wearing a felt collar and silk ribbon tie, stuffed with pellets for weight. 2008/09 13in (33cm) high* ☆☆

Beverly White

Formerly a nurse by profession, Pennsylvanian Beverley White began to make wooden nursery rhyme dolls in 1984 for her new business 'Happy Tymes Collectibles'. Dolls gave way to teddies in 1985, when White made three bears to accompany Goldilocks and found herself converted to their cause.

Her first limited editions, Ben, Betsy and Thom, were produced in 1986–7, and her first original bear pattern, for 'Say Your Prayers Bear', followed in 1988. These bears had an identifying, embroidered accent line ('worry lines') attached to their eyes, which has remained a characteristic feature of White's bears.

White's studio produces approximately three hundred bears each year and annually develops bear designs for Cooperstown Bears. She has also designed for Walt Disney, The Franklin Mint, Little Gems and the Annette Funicello Bear Company. In 2004 she created 'Alfie', the first annual Theodore Society Club Bear.

In 1998, White launched her own manufactured editions under a new label, Global Designs. The 'Basically Bears' design has continued annually in a variety of 14in (35.5cm) dressed bears and 'Teddies to Go' (a simple bear, panda or bunny designed to be stuffed by its new owner) were created for Global Designs in 2001.

White continues to produce hand-made bears, including her trademark 'Portrait Bears'. Starting with Laurel & Hardy in 1992, she has since created several presidents, Chaplin, Ronald McDonald, Churchill, the Beatles, Smokey Bear and many more.

◀ *An American artist bear, 'Winston Churchill', by Beverley White. 16in (40.5cm) high c2009* ☆☆

◀ *A Japanese artist bear, 'Puu', by Yuki Yamanaka, made of aged viscose, with a gingham patch 'replaced' foot pad, no. 4 from an edition of 10. 2007 8in (20cm) high*
☆☆

"Just knowing that your teddy bear is home waiting at the day's end makes each day happier."

TED MENTEN

◀ *A Japanese artist bear brooch, by Chizu Yoshida, in presentation box. 2002 4in (10cm) high* ☆☆

Museums

UK
The British Bear Collection
Banwell Castle, Banwell
Somerset BS29 6NX
www.thebritishbearcollection.
co.uk

The Dorset Teddy Bear Museum
Teddy Bear House
Dorchester, Dorset DT1 1BE
www.teddybearmuseum.co.uk

Hamilton Toy Collection
111 Main Street, Callander
Perthshire FK17 8BQ
Tel: +44 (0) 1877 330004

The London Toy and Model Museum
21-23 Craven Hill
London W2 3EN

Museum of Childhood
42 High Street
Edinburgh EH1 1TG
Tel: +44 (0) 131 529 4142

Park House
Park Street, Stow-on-the-Wold
Gloucestershire GL54 1AQ
www.thetoymuseum.co.uk

The Teddy Bear Museum
Polka Theatre,
240 The Broadway
Wimbledon, London SW19 1SB
www.teddybearmuseum.com

Teddy Melrose Museum
High Street, Melrose
Roxburghshire TD6 9PA
Tel: +44 (0) 1896 823854

The Toy and Teddy Bear Museum
373 Clifton Drive North
Lytham St Annes, Lancashire
FY8 2PA
Tel: +44 (0)1253 713705

The V&A Museum of Childhood
Cambridge Heath Road
London E2 9PA
www.vam.ac.uk/moc

USA
The Teddy Bear Castle Museum
203 South Pine,
Nevada City, California 95959
Tel: +1 530 265 5804
www.teddybearcastle.com

Teddy Bear Museum of Naples
2511 Pine Ridge Road
Naples FL 33942

GERMANY
Margarete Steiff Museum
Alleenstraße 2
89537 Giengen/Brenz
+49 7322 1311
www.steiff.com

SWITZERLAND
Spielzeugmuseum
Baselstrasse 34
CH-4125 Richen

Puppenhausmuseum Basel
Steineck-Stiftung
Steinenvorstadt 1
CH-4051 Basel
Tel: +41 61 225 95 95
www.puppenhauemuseum.ch

JAPAN
Izu Teddy Bear Museum
413-0232
Ito Shi
1041-56 Izukogen
Tel: +81 557 544485

Acknowledgements

Bébés et Jouets
Tel: +44 (0) 1289 304802
bebesetjouets@tiscali.co.uk
63, 66-7, 92, 97-8, 100, 104, 127, 138, 167, 177, 185, 196, 207, 225-6, 232

Calico Teddy
Tel: +1 410-433-9202
www.calicoteddy.com
11, 14, 18-9, 24, 41, 48, 58-9, 57, 60, 62, 218

Kay Cox Private Collection
12, 17, 47, 54, 56, 68, 82, 109, 147-8, 154, 189, 224, 230

Dreweatts
Baverstock House, 93 High Street, Godalming, Surrey GU7 1AL, UK
Tel: +44 (0) 1483 423567
www.dnfa.com/godalming
130

Edwina's Friends/Kathy Martin Private Collection
Tel: +44 (0) 118 9776272
www.edwinasfriends.co.uk
4 (top left and middle right), 26, 33, 36, 39, 42, 50-1, 122-4, 126, 128, 151, 164, 171, 184, 188, 194, 205-6, 216, 222, 234

Farnham Antiques Centre
27 South Street, Farnham, Surrey GU9 7QU, UK
Tel: +44 (0) 1252 724475
49, 149, 160, 186, 193, 235

Thos. WM Gaze & Son
Diss Auction Rooms, Roydon Road, Diss, Norfolk IP22 4LN, UK
Tel: +44 (0) 1379 650 306
www.twgaze.com
166

Gorringes
15 North Street, Lewes, East Sussex BN7 2PD, UK
Tel: +44 (0) 1273 472503
www.gorringes.co.uk
21, 181

Leander Harwood
Tel: +44 (0) 1529 300737
4 (bottom left), 6 (bottom right), 25, 30, 37-8, 40, 43-5, 72-3, 76-80, 84-7, 89, 93-4, 96, 99, 103, 106, 112, 115, 118-9, 129, 134-5, 139, 140-4, 146, 150, 155, 183, 190-1, 201-3, 208-10, 212-3, 215, 220, 223, 268-73, 279-82, 299

Sue Pearson
147 High Street, Lewes, East Sussex BN7 1XT, UK
Tel: +44 (0) 1273 472677
www.suepearson.co.uk
131, 156, 204

Sign of the Tymes
Mill Antiques Centre, 12 Morris Farm Road, Lafayette, NJ 07848, USA
Tel: +1 973 393 0065 ext 110
www.millantiques.com/happle
55, 64, 198, 227

Sotheby's
34-5 New Bond Street, London W1A 2AA, UK
Tel: +44 (0)20 7293 5000
www.sothebys.com
4 (top centre), 20, 35, 114, 120, 182

The Teddy Bear Chest
Tel: +44 (0) 7913 872721
www.theteddybearchest.co.uk
1, 13, 27, 46, 88, 107, 108, 111, 113, 159, 162, 172, 192, 200, 211, 221, 229

Teddy Bears of Witney
99 High Street, Witney, Oxfordshire OX28 6HY, UK
Tel: +44 (0) 1993 706616
www.teddybears.co.uk
3, 4 (top right, middle left and centre, bottom centre and right), 6 (top right, left), 7, 16, 23, 28-9, 31-2, 34, 69, 74, 75 (x3), 81, 101-2, 110, 121, 132, 145, 158, 163, 165, 170, 174-6, 178, 180, 197, 214, 219, 228, 231, 238-53, 256-67, 274-78, 283-98
246 Rupert Bear ®. © Entertainment Rights Distribution Limited / Express Newspapers 2007

The publisher would like to thank John McKenzie, Graham Rae and Robin Saker for their wonderful photography, and all the people who allowed us to photograph their beautiful bears, especially: Leanda Harwood and Peter Woodcock; as well as Vicky Gwilliam at The Teddy Bear Chest; Kathy Martin; Ian Pout at Teddy Bears of Witney; and Dee Urquhart-Ross at Bébés & Jouets.

Index